Everyman, I will go with thee,
and be thy guide

THE EVERYMAN
LIBRARY

The Everyman Library was founded by J.M. Dent in 1906. He chose the name Everyman because he wanted to make available the best books ever written in every field to the greatest number of people at the cheapest possible price. He began with Boswell's 'Life of Johnson'; his one-thousandth title was Aristotle's 'Metaphysics', by which time sales exceeded forty million.

Today Everyman paperbacks remain true to J.M. Dent's aims and high standards, with a wide range of titles at affordable prices in editions which address the needs of today's readers. Each new text is reset to give a clear, elegant page and to incorporate the latest thinking and scholarship. Each book carries the pilgrim logo, the character in 'Everyman', a medieval morality play, a proud link between Everyman past and present.

Wordsmith

HOW I MADE MY DICTIONARY

Émile Littré

Translated by T.K. Gopalan

EVERYMAN

First published in French as *Comment j'ai fait Mon Dictionnaire* in 1880
This translation first published in 1998 by Cre-A:
This reissued edition first published in India in 2015 by Hachette India
(Registered name: Hachette Book Publishing India Pvt. Ltd)
An Hachette UK company
www.hachetteindia.com

SRD

ISBN 978-93-5195-004-2

Hachette Book Publishing India Pvt. Ltd
4th & 5th Floors, Corporate Centre,
Plot No. 94, Sector 44, Gurugram – 122 003, India

Typeset in Baskerville 10.5 /15

Printed and bound in India by Manipal Technologies Limited, Manipal

MIX
Paper from responsible sources
FSC™ C043100

CONTENTS

PUBLISHER'S NOTE

It was somewhat serendipitous that within a day of a discussion on the importance of lineage and cultural history in publishing, we received a proposal that revealed to us a little-known part of Hachette's own history. It was from a passionate publisher in South India who had embarked on a project about two decades ago and published the first English translation of a remarkable, novella-length essay, *Comment j'ai fait mon dictionnaire* ('How I Made My Dictionary') by Émile Littré. Littré later narrated the whole story in a lecture, which makes a small volume. Cre-A:'s translation was done by Dr T.K. Gopalan, a former career diplomat, who got his doctorate from the University of Paris VI. The translation has been commended for its accuracy by *Dictionaries*, a journal of the Dictionary Society of North America, that described his translation as 'accurate and conveying the original's lively, intense effect...' Cre-A: felt the work deserved much more attention and wanted us at Hachette to publish it. We are of course delighted to do so.

Émile Littré was a much venerated lexicographer from France, who was commissioned by Hachette in 1841 to compile 'A New Etymological Dictionary of the French Language'. Littré, a physician who edited a critical edition in Greek of Hippocrates' works, was a formidable scholar, politician and a philosopher, being the chief disciple of Auguste Comte. The work, finally started in 1845, took nearly 30 years to complete, during which France went through a great deal of turbulence.

It is fascinating how a study of the history of words throws up such incredibly driven polymaths who are fascinating characters themselves. The best known among them is Dr W.C. Minor (interestingly, again a doctor) who is the subject of the bestselling *Professor and the Madman*. Littré himself is no less fascinating and, as his short biography that follows shows, led a tumultuous life in the midst of many an intellectual storm. It is equally interesting that he and Charles Darwin are linked in the caricature on page ix. Darwin was also first published by one of the oldest companies in publishing, John Murray, also a part of the Hachette Group, and the two together provide a fascinating glimpse into both a bygone era and a science or art that is forgotten and taken for granted in this day of big data word processing.

This little book is, we believe, a vital philological addition to the study of words and language and an insight into the wonderful men who made that study possible by embarking on such epic ventures.

Caricature of Émile Littré and Charles Darwin depicted as performing monkeys breaking through gullibility ('*credulité*'), superstitions, errors, and ignorance.

Illustration by André Gill, *La Lune Rousse,* 1878.

TRANSLATOR'S NOTE

THE text of this translation follows the French edition published by Editions Bernard Coutaz (1992), which is said to conform to the version of the Didier Edition (Paris, 1880), a collection of articles entitled *Études et glanures.*

The footnotes indicated by a letter are those of that edition. Those indicated by a number are by Jacques Cellard. The translator's footnotes are indicated by a dagger (†).

The note by Pierre Larousse on Émile Littré is extracted from his *Grand Dictionnaire Universel du XIXe siècle* (1864–1884) ('The Great Universal Dictionary of the 19th Century').

This is the first English translation of this work.

ÉMILE LITTRÉ: A BIOGRAPHICAL NOTE

ÉMILE Littré (1 February 1801–2 June 1881) was a French lexicographer and philosopher, born in Paris. Best known for his *Dictionnaire de la langue française*, commonly known as 'The Littré'. His father, Michel-François Littré, was a sergeant-major in the French navy deeply imbued with revolutionary ideas of the day. After settling down as a tax collector, he married Sophie Johannot and devoted himself to the education of his son Émile, who was sent to the Lycée Louis-le-Grand, where he became friends with Louis Hachette, founder of the Hachette publishing company. After Littré completed his studies, he devoted himself to mastering the English and German languages, classical and Sanskrit literature, and philology, before becoming a student of medicine in 1822. In 1827, after the sudden death of his father, he abandoned his degree despite his keen interest in medicine, and began teaching Latin and Greek to earn a living. He fought on the side of Charles X in the July Revolution of 1830 that marked the shift in France to constitutional monarchy. In 1831, he obtained an introduction to Armand Carrel, the editor of *Le National*, who tasked him with reading English and German papers for excerpts. In 1835, Carrel discovered Littré's skills as a writer and from that time on, he was a constant contributor to the journal, eventually becoming its director.

In 1839, the first volume of Littré's complete works of Hippocrates appeared in print. Due to the outstanding quality of this work, he was elected to the Académie des inscriptions et belles lettres – a society dedicated to the study of humanities – in the same year. He came across the works of Auguste Comte, the reading of which formed, as he himself said, 'the cardinal point of his life'.

From this time forward, not only did positivism affect his own life, but more importantly he influenced positivism, giving as much to this philosophy as he received from it. He soon became a friend of Comte, and popularized his ideas in numerous works on the positivist philosophy. He continued translating and publishing his edition of Hippocrates' writings, which was not completed until 1862, and he published a similar edition of Pliny's *Natural History*. After 1844, he was elected to the committee engaged to produce the Histoire littéraire de la France, where his knowledge of the early French language and literature was invaluable.

Littré started work on his great *Dictionnaire de la langue française* in 1844, but it took him 30 years to finish it. In between, he participated in the July 1848 revolution, and in the repression of the extreme Republican Party in June 1849. His essays, contributed during this period to the *National*, were collected together and published under the title *Conservation, Revolution et Positivisme* in 1852. In 1863, after completing his translations of Hippocrates and Pliny, he set to work in earnest on his great French dictionary, which was finally completed in 1873. The draft was written on 415,636 sheets, bundled in packets of a thousand, stored in eight white wooden crates that filled the cellar of Littré's home. Thc landmark effort gave authoritative definitions and usage descriptions to every word in the French language till the time, based on the various meanings it had held in the past. When it was published by Hachette, it was the largest lexicographical work on the French language at that time.

In 1875, Littré was elected senator for life of the Third Republic, and his most notable writings during these years were his political papers, his re-editions of many of his old articles and books, and a little tract, *Pour la dernière fois*, in which he maintained his unalterable belief in the philosophy of Materialism.

Littré published *Comment j'ai fait mon dictionnaire* in 1880, just a year before his death.

About the translator: T.K. Gopalan, a former career diplomat, is a specialist in data analysis. He has a PhD in statistics from the University of Paris VI. He has to his credit translations of research materials in correspondence analysis originally published in French.

ACKNOWLEDGEMENTS

ERIC Auzoux, director, Alliance Française of Chennai, who introduced us to this text and who clarified many of its finer points;

T.S. Nayar, who exhaustively and critically reviewed the translation;

Editions Philippe Picquer for permission to translate and publish the afterword by Jacques Cellard.

CAUSERIE

NOTHING had particularly prepared me for an enterprise of this kind... Nothing? What about the works included in the present volume[1] and the greater ones, contained in the *Histoire de la langue française* ('History of the French Language')? No doubt; but these, which amply qualified me for the transformation of my initial, vague project, came later; and I repeat in all truthfulness: nothing had prepared me for an enterprise of this nature. I was past forty; Greek medicine occupied me entirely, except for a few literary excursions which appeared in dailies and periodicals. I was preparing, for publication by J.B. Baillière, an edition of Hippocrates in Greek, the text having been prepared after a collation of all the manuscripts I could procure, along with notes and commentaries, the first volume of which got me elected to the *Académie des inscriptions et belles lettres* ('Academy of Inscriptions and Belles Lettres'), and the tenth and last volume of which appeared only in the year 1860. It was quite a fair amount of work. La Fontaine[†] says of his man already in possession of sufficient game:

---

[1] *Études et glanures* ('Studies and Gleanings'), of which this *Causerie* is only a part.

[†] The celebrated French poet and fabulist (1621–1695), best known for his *Fables*, modelled on Aesop.

Any modest hunter would have been content with it

His hunter was not modest, and the story teller adds at once:

But what! Nothing fills
The vast appetites of a maker of conquests.

Let us understand however what my *vast appetites* were. I am one of those restless or beguiled minds who would like to scour the diverse fields of knowledge and obtain, to use Molière's fine expression, *some light on every subject*, but, miserly and greedy at the same time, I liked to let go of nothing. It is thus that I continued my Hippocrates, even while starting on my dictionary. What all did I not turn over in my mind? Had I been strong in my old age, had I not been afflicted by sickness, I would have put my hand, with some collaborators, to a universal history for which I had a complete plan.

But let us get back to the subject. In such circumstances, the conception of the dictionary was due to a fortuitous occasion, and had at first only a small beginning and a fragmentary character, and only by successive elaborations did it turn itself into a general plan and into a whole into which all the parts concurred. My readings, always very varied, had exposed me to etymological research. Following this, I amused myself by dividing some French words into prefixes, suffixes and radicals. This appeared curious to me; and forthwith, taking neither the time nor the trouble of carrying the experiment further, I imagined that there was matter in it for an etymological dictionary of the language, redoing, in the light of modern methods, what Ménage[1] had done, not without merit, two hundred years earlier. Besides, these preliminaries, which at first absorbed all my attention and which later shrunk on their own to their true proportions, were not completely wasted; in the final work, I have given a certain place to the prefixes and the suffixes, in their alphabetical order, explaining their origins and meanings; this innovation is not without use, for the prefixes and the suffixes are elements of the French language and knowledge of these matters in the analysis of words.

I proposed my plan to Monsieur Hachette[2] the great bookseller, who was an old friend from school days. He accepted it. The title of the work was to be: *Nouveau dictionnaire étymologique de la langue française* ('A New Etymological Dictionary of the French Language'). A contract was concluded between us. He

---

[1]Gilles Ménage (1613–1692), scholar and wit, author, among others, of *Les Origines de la langue française* ('The Origins of the French Language') (1650) and of *Observations sur la langue française* ('Observations on the French Language') (1673), which were considered authoritative for a long time.

[2]Louis-Christophe Hachette (1800–1864), founder of the publishing house of his name.

advanced me four thousand francs[1]. This was in 1841.

Five years went by without my taking in hand the work for which I had taken the initiative and the responsibility. It was, I agree, too much of a delay and too much negligence. I cannot justify myself, I can only apologise and plead extenuating circumstances. At this time, I had the misfortune of losing my mother. Her death plunged me into a profound mourning and, for months on end, I remained incapable of resuming the normal and necessary routine of my occupations. I say 'necessary', for this sloth, due to grief, brought a lot of discouragement into my affairs. Further, when I began to come to my senses, Monsieur Baillière, the other publisher who was always well disposed and friendly towards me, pressed me for Hippocrates, the successive volumes of which he wanted, rightly, to appear with some regularity. Under these various pressures, I was not able to devote my time to the etymological dictionary, a new work which had to be introduced into my daily schedule, and I neglected my commitments, whose recollection sometimes gave me an unpleasant start.

Monsieur Hachette drew me out of this torpor, which had lasted only too long, and insisted that I begin. We know that occasionally, during sleep, ideas which preoccupied us just prior to it take final shape unconsciously; similarly,

---

[1]That is, in terms of purchasing power, about 250,000 francs now. At that time, a monthly salary or income of 250 gold francs was just right for living comfortably.

during this too long suspended animation of our project, his ideas and mine had changed, and he proposed cancelling our earlier agreement, concluding a new one, and giving the work a new title, the title of *Dictionnaire étymologique, historique et grammatical de la langue française* ('Etymological, Historical and Grammatical Dictionary of the French Language'). The addition of *historical* will be remarked. This was, indeed, ever since I considered my project under all its aspects, the dominating thought which preoccupied me and corresponded best with my scholarship and my position as a member of the Academy of Inscriptions. I was not the first to have thought of the introduction of history in a lexicon of the French language. Voltaire had proposed an outline of it, advising that sentences drawn from the best writers should be quoted instead of arbitrary examples. But it was Génin[1], a lover of the old language, who recommended that one go back deliberately to it, and not be afraid of seeking authorities therein. I appropriated both Voltaire's and Génin's views, out of which I composed an original plan that was all my own. I was the first to attempt subjecting all aspects of the dictionary to history, executing the task if I had the strength, patience and good luck.

See how indeed luck operates. Much later, and when I had already begun the printing, I learnt indirectly that

[1]François Génin (1803–1856), author of *Des variations du langue française depuis le XIIe siècle* (1843) ('Variations of the French Language since the 12th Century').

a learned man, Monsieur Godefroy[1], had also thought of a historical dictionary of the French language and collected material to this end. The news of the lead that I had taken over him made him lose all hope. He was not lucky. However, all was not lost. His vast readings and his rich collection of examples from the old language readily furnished enough material to make a dictionary of the *langue d'oïl*[†], which we needed. Soon I got in touch with Monsieur Godefroy, and I gave my approval for such an enterprise; I convinced him in his belief that it was very much desired; I exhorted, I pressed, I put forward time and again my example and my procedures. Busybody, one would say. Not quite; for Monsieur Godefroy *paid me for my trouble* by dedicating to me his book, whose first fascicle has just appeared, thus robbing German scholarship of the honour it had been merrily preparing for, of giving us French a glossary of our old language[a].

---

[1]Frédéric Godefroy (1826–1897), philologist, author of the monumental *Dictionnaire de l'ancienne langue française, du IXe au XVe siècle* ('Dictionary of the Old French Language, from the Ninth to the Fifteenth Century'), in 10 volumes (1880–1902).

[†]*langue d'oïl*, Old French (as spoken in the North of the Loire).

[a]*Le Dictionnaire de l'ancienne langue française et de tous ses dialectes du neuvième au quinzième siècle* ('The Dictionary of the Old French Language and of All Its Dialects from the Ninth to the Fifteenth Century'), by Frédéric Godefroy, carries indeed this dedication: 'To my dear and respected Master, Monsieur E. Littré, I offer my most affectionate respect and deepest gratitude.' This great work (1880–1895) consists of no less than 8 volumes. The author is preparing a supplement to it which is no less extensive. The *Académie des inscriptions* has honoured this work with the *Gobert Grand Prix*.

To me luck came in the form of the second proposal of Monsieur Hachette. Perhaps, after so many preliminaries, I shall astonish my reader by confessing to him that, far from eagerly grabbing it, I asked for twenty-four hours of reflection. These twenty-four hours were a time of anxiety for me; I passed the night without closing my eyes, weighing up in my mind the burden which I must carry irrevocably. Never did the harsh reality of the lines of Horace[b] come more intensely to my mind. The length of the undertaking, which, as I had foreseen it, would take me into my old age, and the necessity of combining it, during a number of years, with the work by which I earned my livelihood, came in the way of my resolution. Finally, towards the morning, my courage got the upper hand. I was ashamed to withdraw after having come forward. The lure of the plan which I had conceived proved to be stronger, and I signed the agreement.

However, my confession is not quite complete. I have said that Monsieur Hachette had advanced me four thousand francs, and returning that advance became my first obligation, since nothing was concluded between us. I was not incapable of paying it back, but the money was part of some savings to which I was attached like a small saver to his savings. It was not, therefore, without some influence on my decision. All the same, I was not

---

[b]... *Quid ferre recusent,*

Quid valeant humeri.

('Why refuse the burden when one can carry it?')

destined to enjoy it. The February revolution that came two years later[†] robbed me of it, with the rest of those savings which were so dear to me, placed in deposits which were wiped out by the universal credit crisis. The catastrophe did not affect my dictionary, my plan, my resolution. The result (for one must certainly judge by the result since we cannot gauge the future beforehand) gave me much more than what, in my most ambitious expectations, I was hoping by way of compensation.

The beginning was to collect together a good number of examples from our classics and from the texts of the old language. The classics of course, without my having to restrict myself from going beyond them; as regards texts of the old language, I took the most celebrated ones in each century from the twelfth (the eleventh has very little to offer) to the sixteenth included. The sixteenth century is the limit of my historical coverage. My work group was soon constituted. Monsieur Hachette put at my disposal well-read persons who read the authors for me, and wrote down, on small sheets of paper, having at the top the word of the example, the sentences they had picked up. I have cited these persons in the preface of the dictionary and thanked them, as well as some volunteers who were happy to help me. My instructions were very general: to collect, as much as could be done, examples of all the words (despite our searches more than one

---

[†]i.e. in 1848, when King Louis-Philippe was dethroned and the Second Republic was established.

word has remained without a citation), not to omit either archaisms, or neologisms, or infringements of grammar: to look out for oblique or odd acceptations, and to give preference to the examples that were interesting either for their elegance, or for their anecdotes, or for their history. Such were the points which I discussed with them, leaving the execution to their own views, to their habits, to their personal taste and also to chance discoveries.

On my part I read and examined in detail certain books, not only to contribute to the amount of work, but above all to have for myself the experience of this kind of work and to appreciate better the contributions of my assistants. In any case, the true touchstone was the use of these examples and their incorporation into the composition of the entries to which they referred. At that point I realised that several, whether they came from my collection or from those of my assistants, were suspect for various reasons. Monsieur Hachette wanted that I should confine myself to naming only the author of the citations and should not give additional information which would enable one to find them: edition, chapter and page. His motive was that, given the vast number of indications and the ease with which a mistake could occur either while writing down a number or while printing it, the dictionary would be a storehouse of errors. Such was his expression. But even if I had accepted this decision, by far too radical, it would not have remedied what was incorrect or insufficient in certain citations. The only solution was verification every time some suspicion arose, and this was highly laborious, very time-consuming and required a great deal of investigation. Nevertheless I was not put off, and I succeeded in giving my citations all their quality of precision. In spite of Monsieur Hachette's forecast, the dictionary did not become a storehouse of errors.

While I was peacefully collecting examples, terrible events erupted, which changed the face of France. In 1848 a riot, quickly transformed into a revolution, changed it into a republic. The stupefaction, not too benevolent, of the provinces at a change on which they had not been consulted, the revolutionary ideas of some, and the socialist systems of the others, and, among the victors, the uncertainty over the outcome of such a crisis, threw into disarray the public and private fortunes. The bloody conflict of June in Paris itself, between the National Assembly and the workers of Paris, was destined to amend nothing; and when Monsieur Hachette, commanded with his company of the *garde nationale* (National Guard) to attack, on a Friday, a barricade erected in his locality (he was then residing in rue Pierre-Sarrasin, which has since been demolished), received a volley which covered him with the blood of several people near him, it is not surprising that he should have hesitated to continue with such an onerous enterprise as the dictionary, and suspended during the storm the assistance that he was providing me. But the firm was from that time solidly established, and its intrepid and clever chief withstood the circumstances. After what was only a momentary hesitation, he persevered, and I persevered with him.

After a time, the collection that I was making increased so much in volume that I considered that I had provided myself sufficiently with examples. As a matter of fact, it was not the case, but I did quite well to stop the work of collection, subject to resumption. Given the proportions which I had conceived for my dictionary, I would have been lost without any resources of time and space if I had let myself give in to the very natural temptation of making each of the sections of the dictionary comprehensive. It was urgent to resign myself to a sacrifice and go on to the whole by refusing to give finishing touches to the parts. I did not have to regret my decision. The whole was accomplished; that was the essential; for in many cases, it is the supreme judge of the parts. Thereafter the parts were taken up separately and with a better understanding, which compensated sufficiently for the interruption which I had imposed on them.

I recall that some years ago an Englishman, wanting to do for his language what I had done for mine, asked me through an intermediary to apprise him of the manner in which I had proceeded. I wholeheartedly gave him some essential indications; but, I admit it only too readily now, they were certainly insufficient; and if I had then been able to give him the note that I am writing presently,

I would have been more useful to him in sparing him a lot of trial and error that I had to go through myself. I had, it is true, illustrious predecessors in lexicography; Henri Estienne, Du Cange, Forcellini; Du Cange above all, whom I was leafing through constantly, and to whom I am grateful, as if he had been there, listening to me. I do not have the presumption to compare myself with them. Their task, moreover, had not been the same as mine; for they concerned themselves with dead languages wherein everything is closed, whereas I was dealing with a living language in which everything is open. However that may be, they have not told us how they proceeded to compose *their Treasuries*†. I shall be less discreet and, at the risk of being considered less modest, more personal or, to use an English expression, more *egotist,* by my reader, continue my lexicographic narration.

So I put an end to the collection of examples. They were written on little squares of paper, each carrying the name of the author, the title of the work, the page or the chapter. Each writer was represented by a packet of these square slips, already arranged in the alphabetical order. This had to be transformed into a general alphabetical order. This entirely material work, which I took upon myself, kept me busy for many hours a day during more than three months. One can judge by that how

---

†A play on words, giving one of the meanings of the Latin word, *Thesaurus,* which was the title under which many dictionaries and encyclopaedias were then published.

considerable the volume of work was. I truly admired it; not without some secret fright, as I saw it loom so large in front of me. But my trouble was beginning to pay off; for in this heap of small papers, I possessed, in a nebulous state, it is true, the collection of authorities in the classical language and that of the history of the entire language.

I have, in the preface to my dictionary, given the table and the explanation of the mode according to which I have treated each word in particular, and of the constant order that I have followed in this treatment, in such a way that anyone making a search would never lose his way. This table, which I have just read again, is excellent; and if it had been possible for me, and this is my perpetual complaint, to have had it for consultation earlier, it would have spared me the loss of very many hours, and also some anxious periods. But, far from being an antecedent, it was a consequence; and I only obtained it in this clear and precise form at the price of many an aborted trial and many a false route. He who looks at my four volumes, their thousands of pages and their three columns, certainly reckons that a lot of time has been spent on all this; but what he does not suspect is how much time, of which no trace remains, has been buried away in vain and fruitless investigations, in retracing one's steps, in amendments and in revisions.

Less prepared than I thought, but nevertheless sufficiently prepared not to lose my way, I began the compilation and brought it to conclusion. It was long, and

I spent on it not months, but years. The result was a work, not a small one, which appeared definitive to me in my ignorance of myself and my mental conditions. I did not know then as well as I do now, that with me the definitive is not obtained so easily. How much my premature satisfaction was to be chastised! And how far away I was from the end that I believed to have already reached! This mass of paper was going to be doubled, tripled, perhaps quadrupled. I did not keep an exact account, but the fact is that this first compilation disappeared like an embryo into the second.

My disillusionment came into play when at last I had to give the copy (this is the technical term) to the press. All the authors do not behave in the same manner with regard to the copy. Some hand in the copy already in its final shape; it is finished at the first go itself, and as perfect as each one's talent can make it; the proofs get only typographical corrections from them. They are the joy of the compositor, causing no alterations or delays. Auguste Comte and Armand Carrel[1], among those that I have seen at work, have been models in this manner of working: everything was so fixed in their mind that they changed nothing any more, whether it was the thought or the turn of phrase or the expression. Others see in the proof only a draft that can be hewn and altered at

---

[1]Armand Carrel (1800–1836), journalist, was the founder of and driving force behind *National* (1830), the organ of Republican resistance to the Monarchy of July.

will, and they hew it and alter it. A new proof arrives, and it is another occasion to begin the work of correction, and they finally manage to satisfy themselves only at the cost of several proofs, and the curses of the typographer. Lastly there are others who take the middle ground: they are neither as clear-headed as the former, nor as indecisive as the latter. I belonged to this third category, with however a tendency to let go from my hands a copy that was not sufficiently prepared. But, one day when I had erased and revised a copy a lot, Monsieur J.B. Baillière, who was for my Hippocrates what Monsieur Hachette was for my dictionary, remarked that these erasures and amendments were wasted work, tedious for the printer and costly to the publisher, and that it would be preferable for everyone to give the copy a better finish, and to confine 'the revisions to unavoidable cases. The reasoning appeared to me to be irrefutable: and as I am open to correction, having understood early that it was not very wise to reply to a suggestion for improvement with : 'I'm like that', I have ever since set my heart on bringing my copy as near as possible to its final form, to the best of my ability, before I sent it out. It was what I believed I had done in respect of what I shall call the first handwritten edition of my dictionary: but, even so, it was no more than a framework.

Instinctively, that is to say, in the grip of a vague fear of being inadequate to my task, I put off the commencement of printing. On the contrary, Monsieur Hachette was in a hurry to get under way an operation which must last a good many years. He was also negotiating with a university professor who was inclined to collaborate with me, but who, if one put off the beginning too much, would seek employment elsewhere for his few leisure hours. This was Monsieur Beaujean, presently inspector of schools. The rest of my narrative will show how right and farsighted Monsieur Hachette was in not letting slip this collaboration for me. From another aspect also, his insistence was highly justified; for it became more and more urgent that an inexorable external necessity should constrain me to call upon all the resources of my mind, and that I should stop retreating before the heaviness of the burden, like the beast of Horace, *iniquæ mentis asellus*[1].

Pushed and pressured, I decided to take in hand my paper properly numbered and well tied into packets, and to prepare the final copy for the press. There was no limit to my despair – the word is no exaggeration – when I became convinced that as things were, I had no way of providing a copy that would be adequate in quantity and quality to a press which was going to consume a lot of it!

I had just begun with the preposition *à* (at, to, by, for, from, in, into, of, on, with) which is the most difficult word I believe in the entire dictionary. The prospect was discouraging. It was that of a printing which would go at

---

[1]'Little unwilling ass.'

a slow pace, so much so that neither I nor my publisher, no longer young, would see its end. The loss would have been great for him; for me it was an immeasurable disaster, no doubt materially, but above all morally. Then I recollected the night of anxiety and insomnia which I had passed when I took the decision which was turning out so bad, and I repented.

The almost inconceivable and highly unfortunate oversight of a very material precaution aggravated my difficulties further. When I took up the material for rereading before delivering to the press, I noticed that I had not taken care to note down each meaning and each example on a separate paper or have it so done by others. And now, with such a copy, how to bring in the classifications, the rectifications and the additions of the enormous mass of material collected subsequently? It was necessary to recopy a great deal; and recopying a great deal in a work in which the writings were so considerable, prolonged a job which was already too long. Hemmed in like this from all sides, I became despondent.

There is nothing like being in a bad situation to have bad thoughts. I tried to persuade myself that my dictionary, imperfect though it might be in this first compilation, scored over the previous dictionaries by its real advantages, and that that should be enough for me. In this way, I proceeded by self-flattery to decide not to persevere and to resign myself, even while seeing the best and the greatest, to the worst and the least... To begin the printing immediately, to press on with it and to finish it in a relatively short time – what a temptation! But also what a fall before my own conscience and before my duty with regard to my publisher!

Hanc demum litem melior natura diremit[1].

My better nature, in effect, put an end to the internal struggle, of which I was at once the seat and the judge. I was ashamed of my weakness. I was ashamed of the flattery by which I was trying to corrupt myself and allay my scruples. I was ashamed of not putting the interests of my publisher on the same level as mine; I was ashamed finally of not executing my plan fully in its total conception, of abandoning the sound and loyal hope of producing, in a field as hackneyed as lexicography, a truly original dictionary, and of earning some gratitude for me from the workers. These reflections and these reproaches gave me back my self-control. And it was a good thing for me. Instructive, curious and historical elements abound in my dictionary. More than once word has come back to me that, looking for a word, the searcher lingered on and continued to read as he would read an ordinary everyday book. I confess that these words never failed to

Titillate the proud weakness of my heart.

---

[1]'A better nature precisely put an end to this debate.'

All this recompense would have been lost, if I had miserably weakened.

Good and honest advice having thus prevailed, I applied all the force of my mind and my courage to overcome the obstacles confronting me. Soon I saw with complete certitude the crux of my problem: to put myself in control of my situation, it was essential – but also enough – to gain a lead over the press, be it only of some weeks, which would enable me without ever stopping or even slowing down the composition, to fill in, as I was making deliveries to my compositor, my outline with all that I had collected, to revise the divisions in the light of my notes and to recast them, without lowering my high ambitions. This lead I had to gain by preparing each week a little more of copy than the press consumed. How I was able to make these little savings which when added together constituted for me a complete working capital is what I shall explain after having shown first in what manner the work of printing (for I had started it intrepidly) was organised in concert with my collaborators.

They were four in number: Monsieur Beaujean, Monsieur Jullien, Monsieur Sommer and Monsieur Baudry. Monsieur Sommer died while the work was in progress, and was replaced by Monsieur Despois; later, the Captain of the Artillery André offered me his help, which I willingly accepted. Such were my regular collaborators, not to mention several volunteers who, one day or another, for one thing or another, graciously provided me much appreciated information. I shall not repeat here the expression of my gratitude. Not that it has diminished; far from it, I feel it more today than at the time itself. I was then experiencing labour pains and the fever of uncertainty; today a well-established success enables me to put my finger on how much they helped me achieve it. In reality, in a work as complex as mine, the more collaborators one has, the more mistakes, imperfections and lacunae one averts, especially when these collaborators are men of great learning, which they place without reservation at the service of collaboration.

Here is how the order of the work was settled between me, my collaborators and my indispensable instrument, the typographer. I would submit a batch of copy to Monsieur Beaujean. He would initial it and send it to the press. But I have not yet said that this press was that of Lahure. Monsieur Hachette had designated it as a great establishment for a great work. At the same time he had made sure of a good compositor and good workers there. When they looked at a first sample of my manuscript, they refused to take it up under the usual conditions of typesetting, and asked for an increase in wages, which was agreed to by Monsieur Hachette. They did not argue their claim citing the bad handwriting, the erasures and the corrections, or the difficulties in reading, but declared that what increased their task and justified their demand was the old French of the historical portions, which could not be typeset easily like the rest. Before formulating their demand, they had submitted the matter to a kind of arbitral council constituted by workers which they refer to as the *Comité* (Committee) and which pronounced in their favour.

In return for the batch of copy, Monsieur Beaujean would receive a first galley which he would correct. From this, the press would prepare a second galley. Monsieur Beaujean would read it, correct it once again, and would write down his observations in the margin. It is this second galley thus annotated that was sent to me. It was constituted by four columns of text, equivalent to the four columns of what is today the dictionary.

This second galley was also sent to my other collaborators at the same time as to Monsieur Beaujean and subjected to their examination. Their observations neglected nothing, from the humble typographical mistake to the highest points of the language, grammar and etymology. More than once I have trembled on seeing from what errors, which had escaped me, I was protected by the scrupulous attention of my revisers.

When I had in hand all this correction material, including at times personal notes that I might have gathered between the time the copy was sent and the time the second galley was received, I put myself to work. I first read the galley for myself without consulting the work of my collaborators, and I corrected it from my point of view. Then I took Monsieur Beaujean, then Monsieur Jullien, then Monsieur Sommer, and after him

Monsieur Despois, then Monsieur Baudry, then Captain André. Everything went well so long as the observations did not need a prolonged examination, or an additional draft, or additions or deletions. But when I encountered observations which raised ticklish questions, or which I could not accept without redrafting my text, then I had to reflect for a long time to take a decision and resolutely act to redraft such and such portion of the impugned article. Nothing was more laborious than the correction of certain of these galleys. You will have an idea when you know that so many times they left my desk only after swelling by a fifth or by a fourth. No doubt the longest was the intellectual work which they required of me; but, shall I add this punctiliousness which, all said and done, was not really punctiliousness? The clerical work was also long, obliged as I was to adjust on the galley notes and pieces of paper, in such a way that the press should be able to find its way in the maze. How many times, when I was at the height of my predicament, did I not say, half-joking, half-serious: 'O my friends, never make a dictionary!' But vain and passing vexation! It is the case for applying the Picardy proverb quoted by La Fontaine in his fable *The Wolf, The Mother And The Child*†:

> Handsome, gentle wolves, do not hearken
> To mother scolding her son who cries.

---

†The wolf in the story heard a mother telling her crying child that she would throw him to the wolf, was stupid enough to confront her to claim the child, and only got killed in the end.

A galley so overcharged necessitated a new one. I therefore asked for it, verified the corrections, and sent the verified copy to Monsieur Beaujean who passed it for make-up. It was a great step: it had cost a lot of labour, a labour which was sometimes very meticulous, sometimes very lofty.

The press was not slow, and the first proofs of the makeup reached Monsieur Beaujean who read it, noted down his observations and sent them to me. My other collaborators, who also received these proofs, did as much. Those who have printed a lot (and I belong to this number: *honni soit qui mal y pense*†. One day Monsieur Wittersheim, printer and Director of the *journal officiel* (official gazette), whom I was thanking for something, remarked that a printer should be gracious to anyone who gave him so much work), those, as I was saying, who print a lot have experienced that a number of things that escape them in the galley become visible in the make-up. Each new arrangement has its light. I was certainly satisfied when this light led me to some worthy correction or addition: but I was even more satisfied if no modification of the printed text was absolutely necessary; for faced with a necessary change, my anxiety began, constrained as I was to stay within the limits of the typeset page, and not to cause revisions that are always difficult and costly, when they exceed the frame of a make-up. Most of the time,

†'Evil be to him who evil thinks.'

I succeeded in this with copious use of editorial devices and strategems, counting the letters that I was removing and the letters by which I was replacing them, and being happy when the total was right. Entire hours were spent on this; but in the end, by sheer dexterity, I made very rare the extreme cases in which the revisions could not be avoided. It is a long time now since I have ceased to resent what this laborious meticulousness cost me by way of efforts, patience, ingenuity and time; for, from a more general point of view, they had not been without use to me in disciplining my mind inclined towards generalities and obliging it to provide itself regularly with facts, big and small.

However careful the press was, these pages were ordinarily too overcharged for me not to be anxious to verify myself if everything was indeed as I had indicated. After this verification, I sent the proofs to Monsieur Beaujean, who thereafter gave the final corrected proofs. Regularly there elapsed a period of two months between the delivery of the copy and the final corrected proofs. The interval was long; but, seeing things fairly, considering through how many hands the proofs passed, and taking into account the views and the suggestions of each one, it will be judged that it was scarcely possible to ask for more promptness either from the press, always supplied with work, or from Monsieur Beaujean, the kingpin, or from me, the general reviser. When the average speed was clearly seen, I could, by making an estimate of the increase in my copy, calculate approximately how many years I would need (for one had to reckon in years) to reach the completion, supposing that there occurred none of those misfortunes from which human affairs are scarcely exempt. I feared sickness for me or my family, the loss of papers misplaced, or a fire; it was war, to which I had not given a thought, which interrupted me.

The printing, which commenced in the last quarter of 1859, finished in 1872. It lasted therefore a little more than thirteen years. In 1859, I was close to fifty-nine years; in 1872, seventy-one. This interval in a human life, long at any age, is relatively much longer towards the end of one's life. However, I passed it without mishap and without slowing down. But the inclemency of fate operated ruthlessly through external events; the war of 1870 made me lose an entire year; I shall say in fairness to me that, in the presence of dangers and disasters to the motherland, I had no thought for the interruption or the ruin (for the worst was very much a possibility) of my work. My preoccupations were elsewhere. Hippocrates, who was my first study, teaches us that a more severe pain deadens a lesser one. The lesser pain was the dictionary, and it was deadened. In reality, if the war year, spent in the inaction of anxiety, is excluded, the printing had taken twelve years.

The interval of two months necessary for the press to bring a batch of my manuscript from the state of copy to the state of 'passed for press' had been my salvation; for it enabled me to have a lead over the press. The condition for the success lay in this that, for each interval of two months, the volume of copy consumed by the press should be less than the volume of copy which I had prepared and put in a satisfactory state. This satisfactory state consisted in interspersing all the material that had been gathered or was being gathered as one went along, according to a fixed plan, to serve me as an abstract of all the patois dictionaries that I could get, and to make use, more fully than I had done, of the vast compendiums of Lacurne Sainte-Palaye[1] and of Pougens[2]; in a word, transform into a definitive text, corresponding on all points to my views, that first draft which, in my presumption, I had imagined sufficient in quantity and quality. It was a lot of work; but my trial and error methods had served me well, compensating me with a great courage which infused me; I proceeded with certitude, and none of this new work was given over to chance nor lost. As I gained the lead in the manner I have indicated over the press, my reserve of copy ready for press increased in volume, and from that time I was sure of remaining the victor in this battle. The press did not have to make extraordinary efforts; it only had to be regular, with its well measured quantity of

---

[1]Jean-Baptiste de Lacurne de Sainte-Palaye (1697–1781) left above all 23 collections of notes and documents which Littré could consult at the *Bibliothèque Nationale* (National Library).

[2]Marie-Charles Pougens (1755–1833) has similarly left collections of interesting notes.

work, and its well trained team, and it was. But for me, it was an extraordinary effort that was required of me every day, and this, over the years. If I had slackened, I would have jeopardised my lead, and fallen into difficulties, or even impossible situations, comparable to the oarsman of Virgil, who is going against the current in a quick-flowing river, and who

si brachia forte remisit,
Atque illum in præceps prono rapit alveus amni[1].
(*The Georgics, I. 202.*)

In order to keep pace with the large and uninterrupted consumption of the press, I needed assistants who would arrange the papers, do the groundwork, remove the difficulties – be they material or extrinsic – and procure me complete mental freedom for properly studying my subject, big or small, according to the importance of the word, and for drafting it in conformity with the general plan, with the documents to which it pertained, with the often multiple divisions which it was advisable to establish therein, and with the considerations – varied, difficult, subtle (for all these could be encountered) – that it suggested. Monsieur Hachette raised no objection to my plans. He would have readily found me assistants for the required services. But another scheme appealed to

---

[1]'If he ventured to lower his arms, the bark would carry him forward into the river with the strong current.'

me more: this was taking as assistants my wife and my daughter who, witness to my perplexities, offered most willingly to come to my help. This domestic arrangement had, compared to the one that would have called in strangers, a superiority which I appreciated very much; these assistants of a new kind were always by my side, questioned me on what they did not understand, and received then and there all the instructions that the course of the work suggested. For this service, Monsieur Hachette put at my disposal 2400 francs per year. Twelve hundred were for my wife and daughter, twelve hundred for me; for all three of us needed a temporary allowance: my wife and my daughter were spending less time on their housekeeping, and I, with the engrossing course of my dictionary, no longer had any time for certain secondary occupations which helped me make, as they say, both ends meet. The *res angusta domi*[1] dominated the situation, and I willingly accepted all its consequences, that is, the work and the economics; the work, subjected all the same to this rule that it never imposed on me a task which I disliked or which was distasteful to me; and the economics, managed as much as possible in such a way that the present was not completely sacrificed to the future. Moreover, this sum of 2400 francs annually was only an advance; it figured in the debt of forty-odd thousands of francs which I contracted with Monsieur Hachette and of which I shall talk later.

[1]'The domestic constraint.'

For my sickly and weak wife, only a limited amount of work was possible and even permitted by the doctor. But my daughter, young and full of ardent enthusiasm, devoted her time from then on to the service of the dictionary. That was easy in the country, where we scarcely received any visitors except on Sundays, which was moreover devoted to rest, except by me who, reserving for my guests the middle part of the day, worked, as usual, in the morning and at night. The difficulty was greater in Paris, where life is more disturbed. Nevertheless, compensating for all, and setting aside time for distractions that were more useful than ever, since the *nulla dies sine linea*[1] of the Latin dictum was practised to the letter, the construction of my lexicographic edifice proceeded with the continuity which alone leads great works to their conclusion. The intermittent spells of vigorous activity, however energetic they may be, matter little in this; what matters is the uninterrupted assiduity.

My work group and I proceeded as follows: I would mark fifteen pages of the *Dictionnaire de l'Académie française* ('Dictionary of the French Academy'): that was the task for fifteen days. In that fashion, I could, on condition of being faithful to my work-schedule, know exactly when I would terminate my recasting. In this first dictionary that I had compiled, and which was no more than a humble sketch, very useful nevertheless, I would take

[1] 'Not a day without a line.'

the portion corresponding to the fifteen pages of the *Dictionnaire de l'Académie,* and put them in the hands of my wife and my daughter. They would transform these pages in such a way that, out of them, I could redact a copy, that is to say, they wrote on as many separate sheets of paper all the accidents of the word, all its acceptations and all its examples. At the same time they had before them some lexicons, among others the great Pougens, in which I had noted in pencil what was relevant to our fifteen pages mentioned above.

This preliminary preparation of the copy did not proceed without its own difficulties relating to the citations which, at times incomplete, obscure, too short or too long, were nonetheless incorporated as such in my framework. I had become much more exacting. In order to remedy the defects on which I was focussing my eyes too much from now on not to hunt them down ruthlessly, it was necessary to search in the works of authors, which were in the hands of my assistants for that purpose. That did not ordinarily require much time; but what took a great deal of time was when the citation was false or vague, for example 'Massillon' or 'Bourdaloue', without anything else. Then I would recall the advice of Monsieur Hachette, who wanted that the dictionary never cite with more precision; but, even though it would not have been too late for me to conform to this advice, I did not persist in my presumptions to a systematic exactness with less firmness. It was my daughter in particular who was given the responsibility of finding these lost or vague citations. Little by little, by virtue of scanning Massillon, Bourdaloue, Molière and the others, she became a good expert in this kind of research, and rarely did she give up, tired of the struggle, trying to lay her hands on the passage which had been incorrectly and insufficiently indicated. A great discoverer of mistakes of all kinds in the citations came to my help: this was one of my collaborators, Monsieur Baudry, my colleague now at the *Académie des inscriptions et belles-lettres.* Working in a vast and well-stocked public library, he would not hesitate to consult the originals, the texts and the tables which he had in hand as soon as he suspected an example, without minding the trouble. He was particularly my guardian angel for determining the editions which, without specifying them, I had made use of thoughtlessly on someone else's word.

I myself took part, for certain texts, in the search for precision. The person who had scanned for me the forty-two volumes of the great edition of Bossuet had indicated, in a manner not easily intelligible to others than himself, several works of the Bishop of Meaux, sermons, little treatises, and some others. Not having with me the forty-two volumes, I wrote down in a notebook the examples to be searched, and on Fridays, which were the days when the *Académie des inscriptions et belles-lettres* was in session, which I was then very regular in attending, and to which today a sickness, painful and without respite, forbids access, I would thumb with curiosity my Bossuet, placed at my disposal by the library of the *Institut*[†]. How many hours were thus consumed by my assistants and myself in investigations many of which might have been avoided by some more precautions while taking extracts from the authors! But, on the one hand, it is difficult for me above all to foresee from afar all the occasions of miscalculations; and, on the other, coming after the event, these retrospective investigations had the advantage of familiarising me usefully with the slightest details of my work. The experience has taught me that nothing is as valuable to me as being obliged to go over meticulously the work already executed.

My biweekly tasks, although materially equal in length to the number of pages taken each time from the *Dictionnaire de l'Académie*, were, in reality, often greatly unequal: unequal, when in the section there was a word with a lot of acceptations. A word with a large number of acceptations was the greatest of the difficulties that I encountered on the way. Two principal causes converged therein. The first lay in the rule that I had given myself, an excellent one which is an original feature of my dictionary, of ranking the acceptations in their natural order, that is to say, by beginning with the most direct and by ending with the most indirect. In these gradations, hardly perceptible or else confused in some aspect, I am

---

[†]Institut de France, the collective name of the five French Academies, of which *Académie des inscriptions et belles-lettres* is one.

not afraid to say that it was necessary to use many acuities of discrimination to respect the real subtleties of the tongue. The second lay in the classification, under each number for a different acceptation, of the examples which also had their ambiguity and their multiple contacts, for they had not been written by the authors for being classified under lexicographic entries, and the nuances of the individual mind, in which they were steeped, impeded the operations – necessarily more general – of the classifier. The alphabetical order required unfortunately that, for my beginning, I had to deal with the preposition *à*, the most difficult word, which I could not handle to my satisfaction. Further on, having acquired more experience and encountering the verb *faire*, which, from this point of view, is scarcely less forbidding, I had better success; and, when one of my good friends, Dr Michel Lévy, Chief Medical Officer of the Val-de-Grâce region and author of a great treatise on hygiene, replying to someone who was praising me for I know not what work, affirmed that nothing equalled, for the degree of the difficulty overcome, to my drafting of the entry in respect of the verb *faire* in my dictionary, I received with intense satisfaction this unexpected attestation, which answered best my apprehensions as well as my hopes. His memory recalls to mind how many very dear friends I have lost, and how many voids have arisen around me; life would be less hard if people grew old together, but let us say no more. My obstinacy to investigate thoroughly everything that appeared suspect, far from weakening, increased with the obstacles. As a consequence, I had to prolong my waking time beyond the habitual 3 a.m., which was my prescribed hour.

This regulation embraced all 24 hours of the day, of which it was essential to spend the least possible time on the usual daily necessities. I had managed, by sacrificing all kinds of superfluous things, to have the luxury of a country residence and a city residence. The country residence was in Ménil-le-Roi (Seine-et-Oise), a small, old house, with a well-planted garden of one third of a hectare, productive in fruits and vegetables, which *dapibus mensas onerabat inemptis*[1], like to the old man of Virgil. There in near-total solitude (for my village is out of the way of the Parisians who escape from the great city on Sundays), it was easy to plan the hours. I would wake up at eight in the morning; it was very late, one will say, for a man so much in a hurry. But wait. While my bedroom was being cleaned, which was also my study (I said it was an old and small house), I went down to the ground floor, carrying some work; it is like this that, *inter alia,* I wrote the preface to my dictionary. The chancellor d'Aguesseau[2] had taught me never to despise what looked like idle moments, he whose unpunctual wife always made him wait for dinner

---

[1]'... provided the tables with free food.'

[2]Henri François d'Aguesseau (1668–1751), Chancellor of France. The account is evidently bookish, no doubt taken from the correspondence of the Chancellor.

and who, presenting a book to her, said: 'Here is the work of the pre-dinner times!' At nine, I would go up and correct the proofs received in the meanwhile up to lunch. At one I resumed my place at work, and there, up to three in the afternoon, I would catch up with the *Journal des savants* ('Journal of Scientists'), which had elected me in 1855, and to which I loved to contribute regularly. From three to six I would take up the dictionary. At six I would go down for dinner, which was always ready; for my wife did not do things like Madame d'Aguesseau. About an hour was enough for it. It is recommended as a hygienic precept not to do office work immediately after meals; I constantly broke this precept, after making an experiment which showed that the infringement did not affect me: This was so much of a gain snatched from the bodily needs. Going back to work about seven in the evening, I would resume the dictionary, and would no longer leave it. The first shift would take me to midnight, when I would be left alone. The second would take me to three in the morning. Ordinarily, my daily task was finished. If it was not, I continued my wakefulness beyond this hour, and more than once, when the days were long, I would extinguish my lamp and continue in the light of the emerging dawn.

But let us not transform the exception into the rule. Most often three in the morning was the time when I would lay down pen and paper, arrange everything in order, not for the next day, for the next day was already arrived, but for the next task. My bed was there, where it almost touched my desk, and in a very few instants, I was in bed. Habit and regularity (this is a physiological observation which is not without interest) had extinguished all the excitation resulting from work. I would sleep as easily as would a man of leisure; and it is thus that I would wake up at eight, the hour of many lazy people. These periods of nocturnal wakefulness were not without some compensation. A nightingale had established its home in a small alley of linden trees, which lies transversally across my garden, and would fill the silence of the night and of the countryside with its limpid and dazzling voice. Oh! Virgil, how could you, author of the *Georgics,* make a mournful song, *miserabile carmen* (a mournful chant), out of these glorious sounds?

In the city, the time was less organised. The day had its visitors coming in and going out and its unexpected disturbances. But in the evenings I would once again be fully in control; my nights belonged to me and I would employ them exactly like in Ménil-le-Roi; winter nights in which I missed my familiar nightingale, and the view of the countryside, and the wide horizon, but which had their silence, even in Paris, when towards two or three in the morning everything became quiet there, and which would pass one after the other while I was immersed in work.

My friend Monsieur Barthélemy Saint-Hilaire[1] has industrious habits no less than mine, but quite different. Winter and summer, he gets up very early in the morning and goes to bed early. So I have said often joking that, if we lived in the same house, we would meet each other on the staircase, he getting up and going to work, and me leaving work and going to bed. Happier than me, he enjoys a vigorous and robust old age, which has not at all changed his active hours and which will enable him to bring to a successful conclusion his great translation of Aristotle. To tell the truth, he is younger than me by four-and-a-half years; and four-and-a-half years ago I was fairly hale and hearty, even though less so than him. I hope this interval of time will bring no disability to him, and that he will remain one of the privileged among the old. Of course, I envy him this well-being in old age; but I shall be very sad if, by some wicked quirk of nature, he stopped deserving from me this kind of envy[a].

From 1860 until the end of the printing, that is for a period of twelve years, I was never wanting in the discipline that I had imposed on myself. I will not say that the impatience to finish did not grip me in certain moments of physical and mental lassitude. But what was

---

[1]Jules Barthélemy Saint-Hilaire (1805–1896), philosopher and politician.

[a]Monsieur Barthélemy Saint-Hilaire died on 24th November 1896, aged ninety-one, having worked until his last day. The translation of Aristotle, mentioned above, had been completed four years prior to this.

fairly remarkable was that this did not happen when the volume of work, barely touched, appeared discouraging by its enormous size, but when it diminished perceptibly and when I was approaching completion. Then I would be irritated by the slowness of the stages which remained for me to go through; I would count and recount the pages to be compiled and the hours that it would require. Then, rebuking myself for my weakness, I would return to the regular course of my days and my nights which had not taken me so far only to let me weaken in the last lap of the road and when the goal was very much in sight. To weaken a little has its compensation: it is the exhortation by the self to the self. Nothing better for supporting oneself with good thoughts and firm purpose than giving oneself from time to time a proper sermon which goes to the heart of things and cuts the character to the quick. Then no preacher can equal us for shutting our mouths and opening our eyes.

There was however an infraction. It was important enough and characteristic enough not to be passed over in silence. At the moment when I began to be fully active in work, in 1861, the widow of Auguste Comte asked me to write her husband's biography, affirming that, considering all the circumstances, I was the one who could write a most well-informed one, and putting at my disposal her recollections and her papers. I refused for a long time, arguing that my dictionary was taking up all my time, and promising to devote myself without reservation, as soon as it was finished, to the work that she was demanding of me, as the duty of a living disciple to a dead master. Madame Comte, with more reason than I believed then, thought that that would be postponing my promise too far. Our discussions regarding this were stormy, for I was aware how very difficult it would be for me to satisfy her, and a rupture between us became imminent. Finally her stubbornness vanquished mine. Her appeals for gratitude to the founder of the positivist philosophy and to this philosophy itself triumphed over my difficulties, which I tried no longer to consider as impossibilities, and I added to the urgency of my dictionary the urgency of this new responsibility which befell me in an unexpected manner.

From then on I had to modify the order of my work and to insert in it the compilation of *A. Comte et la philosophie positiviste* ('A. Comte and the Positivist Philosophy'): it is the title of the work which emerged from my deal with his widow. I judged that it would take me nearly a year for this compilation; and the execution did not prove me wrong. As regards the printing, which lasted about as long, it did not bother me; for the reading of proofs belonged, as I said, to my mornings, and the addition of these proofs was not sufficiently burdensome to upset my schedule. For carrying out the project itself I hesitated between two decisions: either interrupt for a year the recasting of my dictionary – I had sufficient lead over the press for it to leave me this period and not come too soon to dog me again – or else confine myself to decreasing somewhat the hours allocated to the dictionary, and in the time so gained do the life of Auguste Comte. Happily I decided on the latter course. The other would have been disastrous; it would have prolonged by an entire year the already long duration of the printing, and would have postponed the termination to the end of 1873, instead of to the end of 1872. Such a delay would have cruelly affected an old man who had by then exhausted his health and strength.

Having thus decided, I would interrupt my dictionary at midnight, and from midnight until three in the morning I would take up the life of Auguste Comte. These three morning hours (for the astronomical day begins at midnight) taken off the dictionary work regularly without fail during about a year, and combined with the moments that I could pick up here and there, were adequate; in 1863, the volume was ready. During this period I had a somewhat shorter lead over the press in respect of the dictionary, and that was all. The completion of my recasting was only delayed by a few months which, eventually, hardly matters either for me or for the dictionary. But you will have no difficulty in believing that I felt greatly relieved when I reached the end of this tough operation and that I was without anxiety on both issues, that of the book concerning Auguste Comte, and that of the recasting. The result showed that Madame Comte had not presumed too much on my devotion; and when I was out of the fire, I congratulated myself on what had been achieved: the payment of my debt as a disciple had been required, and I had paid it.

My permanent assiduity in work, not letting myself be diverted by any distraction nor by any fatigue, was rewarded, and in 1865 I was able to record on the last page: 'Today I have completed my dictionary.' My equally tireless collaborator, Monsieur Beaujean, who is also a collector, has kept in his possession this autograph, a testimony to a fit of satisfaction which took hold of me at the moment and which I could not prevent myself from recording as I felt it. It was truly finished this time; and a new and presumptuous illusion had not come to dupe me. Ever since, my dictionary received no modification, no recasting. No doubt, while the printing was in progress I was again seeing my copy in the meantime, adding to it, by way of additions and corrections, all that which, in the interval, I had collected or had kindly been communicated to me; but that had no longer any effect on the whole, which remained completely set. From these notes collected during the printing, some naturally referred to what had already been printed and which could no longer be changed. I made a little collection of them, which, under the title of *Supplément* ('Supplement'), amounted to some fifty pages and constituted the closing part of the fourth volume. In the years that followed the publication of the dictionary, this little supplement increased very much in size, and it has become a separately published volume. But who can hope ever to close a dictionary of a living language? Even today I gather without batting an eyelid what my readings or spontaneous correspondents indicate to me as omissions, as lacunae, as errors. Superfluous pains no doubt; for my great age and permanent sufferings forbid me to think of undertaking anything of this nature, but a care which my lexicographer's conscience does not allow me to neglect. That constitutes a provisional file which my successors will find, and which will perhaps not be useless to them, if ever my dictionary is revised into a second edition[a].

I do not know who it was who said that one could think ill of oneself, but that one must never say it, seeing that others would seize it without allowing for extenuating circumstances. I do not subscribe to this opinion either in theory or in practice. It matters little to me if the bad things that I say of me should be repeated, not because of contempt for 'what people will say', but because I want to do some soul-searching; for what I seek above all in saying them is to inculcate into myself more peremptorily what I believe to be the moral necessity of guarding myself, deliberately, against every inadequacy of mine. Applied to my dictionary, this criticism of myself shows that I only conceive my plan as I go along, that the execution is marred by the same defect, and that my ideas and my means take full shape only by a good deal of trial and error. Moreover, that is nothing but a particular instance

---

[a]In 1877, Littré published a new supplement of 375 pages.

of the general defect of my mind, a defect which I have described in my book *Conservation, Révolution et Positivisme* ('Conservation, Revolution and Positivism'), 2nd edition, page 492, and which consists essentially in guessing nothing, in knowing nothing by intuition and, so to say, in advance, and in being obliged to learn everything by painfully acquired experience and by redoubled efforts.

Happily in the great matter of my dictionary, the good parts of myself resisted discouragement and, turning round the words of Ovid:

Video meliora proboque,
Deteriora sequor[1]

they rendered the bad ones ineffective. Therefore when, in 1865, I wrote on the last page what I have narrated above, my conception had reached all the fullness that it implied, and the execution proceeded according to the ideal model.

Ideal? Does this beautiful word belong to the humble and mechanical work of arranging one after the other the words of a dictionary? Well, yes indeed, and I do not retract it. When I had covered the vast development of the French language according to its history, and when it seemed to me that a dictionary could be modelled according to this great image, then an ideal emerged which illumined my work.

---

[1]'I discern and approve the best, I become attached to the worst.'

The recasting, which had immensely swollen the dimensions of the dictionary, had at the same time given it a very special character that barely left it with any resemblance with its predecessor dictionaries. Therefore, in 1863, Monsieur Hachette, who kept himself informed of my views and my plans, considered it appropriate to modify the title on which we had agreed, and which became what it is now. The extent of the book was fixed at two large volumes 4to with three columns, of two hundred to two hundred and fifty sheets each.

The dictionary was getting published as it was being printed, in fascicles of twenty sheets each. It was reckoned that the total would go up to twenty-five fascicles; but there again the forecasts were exceeded. The subject always yielded a little more than what it had seemed to me it would. Not that I indulged in ramblings and inessential superfluities; but, by scrupulously restricting myself within the lines drawn, since I was keen not to omit anything that was essential or shorten anything, the copy became longer under my pen, not without provoking my apprehensions. I was indeed making my way between two preoccupations, between two pitfalls: not to remain less than my framework, and yet not to reach such dimensions as would render the work inaccessible. The result was in my favour. The number of fascicles rose to thirty, which was in no way excessive. The only awkwardness that resulted was this: it was necessary to make some modifications to the contract. It was the son and the successors of Monsieur Hachette who took upon themselves this responsibility; for, alas! Monsieur Hachette, carried away prematurely by sickness, did not see, in its new conditions, a culmination which owes so much to him. What would I have done without a publisher who was such a friend, so devoted, so steadfast, so resolute in the face of misfortunes and difficulties?

I have already said that the firm of Hachette had furnished me various advances. They amounted, in the end, to more than forty-thousand francs. An article of the 1863 contract stated, without any other explanation, that I should reimburse this sum. The reimbursement was self-evident; but I pointed out to Monsieur Hachette that in case as seemed possible to all, and likely to some, the dictionary only achieved a *succès d'estime,* or in other words was not a success and brought nothing either to the publisher or the author, the above-mentioned clause would ruin me completely; for it was to this sum that my savings, made with diligent care, nearly amounted, in order that I may leave, after my death, to my wife and my daughter, the means of a modest living. Monsieur Hachette at once recognised the legitimate nature of my observation. The clause was amended; and it was stipulated that these forty-odd thousand francs would be deducted not from my private assets, but from the sale proceeds of the dictionary. In this way, I and my savings were protected. Success made it easy to reimburse. From the price that the firm of Hachette was paying me for each fascicle, it retained one half, until the extinguishment of my debt; and it was not long before I found myself freed, without in any way having harmed the firm of Hachette, and without having experienced any loss. It is true that this liberation, beneficial to both the parties, depended on the eventuality of success. In case of failure, the loss would have prejudiced the firm of Hachette in respect of its considerable expenditures of all kinds, and me proportionately much more; for all the years that I had devoted to the dictionary would have remained unproductive; and I would have expended enormously in work and sleepless nights only to find myself old, tired and exhausted, having saved from ruin only some little savings that I had not wanted to jeopardise.

After the accomplished fact and the assured sales, some people suggested to me that the firm of Hachette had not treated me with sufficient generosity. I have always rejected such suggestions, replying that not only did I not have any claims, but that I was also satisfied with my share. I am not talking of the clauses of the treaty which binds the contracting parties; they are obligatory, and there it is a question of legal equity; I am talking of a higher equity which would amend them by common agreement. Well, this higher equity itself is not in question. I am very pleased at the apportionment as it has been done, and, to be very pleased about something is more than to acquiesce in it.

The common work of my collaborators and myself, which lasted so many consecutive years, was only interrupted during the holidays. Then everyone went for the distraction that suited him best. I passed one month in Brittany by the sea: at Saint-Quai, near Saint-Brieuc; at Laberbrach, near Brest; at Le Pouliguen, near Saint-Nazaire; at Pléneuf, near Lamballe, but most often at Roscoff, near Morlaix. I would return from these holidays, amply refreshed and fortified, to my cramped residence in Paris. Then winter would come; I would emigrate hastily to my village of Ménil-le-Roi; and there, the open air, the woods, the greenery, the river and the beautiful meadows brought the best joys to my hardworking life.

I had at that time, indeed, in rue de l'Ouest, now rue d'Assas, a very small and very inconvenient flat, but very cheap, as suited my meagre income, the same one that the men of the Commune occupied in May 1871 for three days. From the windows they fired at the soldiers from Versailles, who were entering; thereafter, when, outflanked there as elsewhere, they took flight, they were careful not to leave without setting fire to the ground floor. The house was ablaze; but the Army, arriving, controlled the blaze, as well as the one in the opposite house where Michelet[†] lived – he was happily away at the time – and which the arsonists did not forget. I confess that, at that

---

[†]Jules Michelet, noted French historian, author of the celebrated *History of France* in 6 volumes (1833–1846), and *The French Revolution* in 7 volumes (1847–1853).

instant, I had an intense gratitude to the soldiers from Versailles for having saved my meagre furniture, my books, my papers, my notes and a few cherished souvenirs. But it appears that all that is changed since the return of the amnestied men from Nouméa amidst resounding ovations. The leaders and the chiefs of the amnestied prisoners shout their heads off at us that it is the regular army that was criminal, that the men of the Commune fulfilled a just and proper function by setting fire to houses, palaces, libraries and the town hall, and that the miserable personal interest which made me concerned for my home is what put me and puts me on the side of the oppressors. I had and I retain the most powerful motives, and motives that are more disinterested, for supporting the legal action which, by military strength, suppressed a sinister insurrection and gave Paris back to France. Is this politics? No doubt; and how would a man, whose house was set fire to because of politics, avoid it?

So, in this apartment which the Commune had very nearly burnt, and before the disasters of the siege, Monsieur Hachette, coming to visit me one day, noticed the piles of paper which hindered him, and which were the as yet unprinted part of my dictionary. Their closeness to the fireplace struck him, and the anxiety about a fire came to his mind. 'What could be done', he asked me, 'to safeguard against an irretrievable loss? Would there be a way of copying all this to have a duplicate of it?' I demurred that taking a copy of such a mass would be very long and very expensive, that to the risks at my home would be added the risks at the copyist's, and that, with such a purely subsidiary operation, there was reason to fear delays which it was so important to shorten. The proposal was left hanging. But I remained under the impression provoked by it, and very much concerned about the possibility of a fire. My improvident feeling of security had disappeared; and I thought out some precautions, if not for eliminating, at least for mitigating, mishaps whose flaming picture made me tremble. My manuscript had been arranged into packets of thousand leaves; after a count, I found that I had two hundred and forty of these packets. Consequently, I ordered eight cases in whitewood, with a capacity of thirty packets each, and totally two hundred and forty thousand leaves. It was the concluding part of the dictionary, and represented nearly the equivalent of what had already been printed and saved from possible dangers. These cases were entrusted to a packer, who prepared them as if they had to cross the seas and go to America or India, or in other words resist the passage of time, humidity and all kinds of bad weather. They did not have to travel so far. I carried them over to Ménil-le-Roi, and kept them in the cellar. There the fire did not threaten them any longer so to say. I had a neighbour only on one side, which diminished the risk by half; I lived alone in the house, and also only during the summer season, and I kept clear of the dangers of winter, when fires are particularly frequent. Lastly, if bad luck would have it that it should burn, this house, not very high and of small dimensions, would not by its fall cause the cellar to cave in. The cases remained there several years. The packer had not overestimated the value of his work, and the papers contained in them did in no way suffer from the long stay they made in them. I took them out one after the other as they were needed for printing. It is thus that I arrived at the middle of the terrible year 1870†.

After the initial battles were lost, which only too well announced the inadequacy of our government and of our military chiefs, I understood very soon that the war would arrive at the gates of Paris; for one knew by then that Marshal Bazaine, by an unbelievable and unpardonable negligence, allowed himself to be cut off and surrounded in Metz, and it was thought that Marshal de Mac-Mahon, with the army from the camp of Châlons, would beat a retreat, in order to conserve it for the defence of Paris, which, without it, would certainly be laid siege to and cut off from the rest of France. I was, therefore, convinced that the surroundings of Paris would be the theatre of active military operations, and that the villages within the area, including Ménil-le-Roi, were in danger of becoming positions taken and retaken, and being set fire to. With these prospects such as I had imagined them, and despite the bitter agony of the national misfortune,

---

†Year of the Franco-German war.

I was concerned about my cases, as I should be; for I was not the only one to be interested in their preservation: the firm of Hachette was interested too. I took the cases that remained and carried them to Paris, before the siege.

Well, I was wrong; my cases could have remained at Ménil-le-Roi, without running the risk of perishing with the village which sheltered them. The army from Chalôns, by an inspiration that emanated from the Tuileries† and that was perfectly in line with the entire strategy of a terrified government, let itself be taken *en masse* at Sédan – men, horses, guns, cannons, generals, emperor and all – and no battle took place in the countryside round Paris. Ménil-le-Roi was not occupied by the Germans. They only passed in and out of it. On one of their passages, noticing an uninhabited house, they forced open the door and entered it. The damage was limited to that. I was even told that on entering and seeing my books, they said: 'Nice library.' The fact is that, returning nine months later, in March 1871, I found everything intact; even the clothes that I had left in haste while leaving were still on my bed, in my bedroom, which was also, as I said, my study. In the beginning the inhabitants of Ménil-le-Roi had fled; but soon they returned to their homes. They thought of me, even while I was absent; and, in order to prevent my house from appearing to be uninhabited, and for that reason more

†At the time, the seat of the Executive.

exposed to pillage by the men who were going and coming between Carrière and Maisons-Laffitte[†], they installed one of their men in it. I had been good to them as doctor in their sickness; they were good to me as protectors and defenders of my abandoned home.

In Paris, with my cases, another difficulty arose. It would have been unwise, and contradictory to the kind of precautions that I was seeking, to keep them in the third-floor apartment that I occupied, in rue de l'Ouest, for this apartment was in the range of the German cannons. And indeed, two shells fell there. To tell the truth, these shells (one of which destroyed the furniture of a poor lady neighbour, but on the fourth floor and on the other landing) did not hit me. As soon as communication was reestablished between Paris and Bordeaux, where I was then, a newspaper announced that everything was destroyed in my apartment; but soon reassuring letters informed me that nothing of the kind had happened. All the same, it was not advisable to rely on such unpredictable strokes of good luck.

The odyssey of my cases was not therefore over. I asked the firm of Hachette to keep them, and they agreed. There, these cases were out of the reach of the shells; no projectile coming from the Left bank reached there. They were placed in a very solid basement, where they seemed safe from all damage. It was however in this safe place that they ran one last and serious danger.

[†]Small towns near Paris.

During the retaking of Paris by the Army, which was executing the orders of the legal government of France, a group of people belonging to the Commune occupied one end of the rue Hautefeuille, at the exact point where the publishing house of J.B. Baillière and that of Hachette are situated. When the progress of the troops from Versailles became menacing, these men debated behind their barricades their sinister resolutions, which were put into execution in so many places. They were getting ready to set fire to this group of buildings; but they were interrupted in their plans, wrongly according to them, rightly according to me, by the soldiers, who dispersed them. The buildings of Baillière and Hachette were saved from destruction, and so were my cases.

Delivered from concern for what remained to be printed of my dictionary, I thought of myself and my relatives; and, after much cruel hesitation between my various duties, decided to leave Paris. I could not, given my age, take part in its defence, and I thought of rendering a negative service by taking away some unproductive population (which many others ought to have done, too) from a city which was going to be besieged and hungry. All my habitual social contacts outside of my home were in Brittany. It is there that we – myself, my wife and my daughter – took refuge. We found cordial hospitality at the home of Dr Fortmorel at Saint-Brieuc, and our exile was mitigated. But how lengthy did the days seem to be! We would hanker after each day's newspaper, which brought good news only once, that of the battle of Coulmiers; we received by balloons some letters which informed us of our friends, of Paris, of its sufferings, and of the generous endurance of the Parisians; and we bitterly reproached ourselves for eating our bread so comfortably, while they were advancing every day towards their last resources. In this unproductive wait, and to kill the time which was killing me, I made use of Dr Fortmorel's library, and I collected some material for my dictionary, even though in the darkest hours, I did not know any more if we would at all have a motherland and all that this sacred word implies. No distress seemed impossible, especially to an old man who hardly believed any more that he could go back to his life and work again.

At last, lights appeared in the sky that was so dark. The National Assembly, of which eighty-thousand Parisian electors had made me a member, moved to Versailles. But the gates of Paris did not yet open for me. The city was busy with the insurrection of 18th March†; and, once the siege began, I could not return there. There were other anxieties: with such a small number of troops, which Monsieur Thiers had at his disposal, troops who were so much disorganised, and disheartened, nothing

---

†The second *Commune* of Paris was the revolutionary government (18th March–27th May, 1871), installed in Paris after the lifting of the siege of the city by the Prussians and overthrown as a result of a new siege of the city by the regular army of the Government headed by Thiers with its provisional seat in Versailles.

was more uncertain than the fight against the revolting Parisian populace, large in number, who controlled all the forts except the one on Mount Valérien, and who were formed into battalions and provided with unlimited quantities of guns, cannons and ammunition. Despite the circumstances being so unfavourable, and despite my having almost no heart for the work, Monsieur Beaujean, who remained in Paris, and who was able to serve as my intermediary, insisted in a pressing manner that we resume the work on the dictionary, interrupted since nearly a year. And he was truly inspired in forcing my hand in this way; there was, as I soon realised, nothing to be lost by resuming, and much to be gained, that is to say, time, confidence in a reversal of luck, and work on a restoration which it was everyone's duty to start without delay. My collaborators showed themselves to be quite ready. The press received the copy with satisfaction, and the workers came back to compose it. At Hachette's the particular one of my cases was opened on which they had been working at the time of the interruption. Everything in it had slept for long months; but as in the story of Perrault[†], everything – copy midway, galleys half-corrected and sheets begun – woke up with a start.

The proofs were sent not without difficulty to Versailles and not without difficulty returned to Paris.

[†]Charles Perrault, French writer (1628–1703). His celebrity comes from his stories for children (*Contes de ma mère l'Oye,* 1697).

My greatest trouble came from my separation from my lexicographic apparatus. But this trouble did not last. The insurrection failed, and I returned to Paris, to my work, to my books and to my entire installation. From then on the printing progressed fast, and it was completed in 1872, at the end of the year. I have recorded above what deep-seated joy I experienced in 1865, when I wrote the last page of the revision. The final print order that I gave in 1872 revived with no less liveliness the feeling of an accomplishment obtained with great efforts, after many years, despite moments of true inner despair and very hard external obstacles.

These last eighteen months (1871–1872) were inordinately busy and difficult for me. All the regulations of my life for procuring for myself the greatest amount of free time were upset. As member of the National Assembly, I attended its sessions regularly. Not being able to take up residence at Versailles because of my books and because of what I was doing in Paris, I was obliged to make every day the journey about which so many complaints have been made and which has only just now ceased. In that way, the middle parts of the days were entirely taken away from me; only the mornings, the nights, the Sundays and the Assembly vacations remained for me. One can imagine without difficulty with what intent care I used these hours taken away from public duties, and how much I rejoiced when I found them adequate.

It was at the end of this year 1872 that my health began to deteriorate profoundly. I had frequent attacks of fever; a catarrh settled in the nasal and respiratory tracts and has not left me ever since; the nails of my hands became ill and fell off one after the other. Neither time nor medical treatment brought any relief: time, on the contrary, aggravated day by day the burden of old age; medical treatment found no support from a constitution falling in ruins. And indeed, my condition, far from improving, after a painful but bearable phase, became complicated with the onset of rheumatism, which caused and is causing me great pain, and which also has taken on the permanent character of the earlier and still persisting troubles. Little by little I became totally confined to my room, almost nailed to my armchair, and I portrayed fairly well the wretched Scarron[†] whom we know, with somewhat less infirmity perhaps, but surely with a stubborn catarrh in addition, conserving like him the lucidity of mind, and using it, like him, for the distractions of intellectual work. I have attentively examined, from the medical point of view, if I could legitimately put down the sufferings which are afflicting me at the end of my existence to the kind of life I have led during the last fifteen years of my dictionary; and it was impossible for me to see in it any cause-and-effect relationship. A lot of people have worked

[†]Paul Scarron, French writer (1610–1660), stricken with paralysis in 1638. He is the author of burlesque poems including *Le Virgile travesti.*

and are working as much as I did without becoming prey to the complicated sickness which has taken hold of my person. My ill health did not at all occur gradually, as would be the case if it had been caused by a progressive overworking; it invaded me at once and, as regards the final rheumatism which added itself to it and made me the sad match of the author of *Le Virgile travesti*, they say that the poor devil owed his sickness to an imprudent practical joke which exposed him without protection to the influence of cold. Considering the history of my sickness, I am disposed to blame an unfortunate heredity, both in respect of my rheumatism as well as in respect of what preceded it. My paternal grandfather, although he died very old (eighty-nine years), was tormented for many years by gout; my father, who lived much less, had attacks of gravel, to one of which he succumbed; and it is known medically that gout and gravel are related. For my part, I am racked by general disorders and disorders of the humours, and above all by rheumatism which is also related to the inclination to gout. I therefore clear the dictionary of all suspicion of having brought about all the organic disorders which afflict me.

The sickness, which has never left me, caused me at the time of completion, with which its onset coincided, a disappointment, small no doubt, but which was palpable to me. My plan was to entertain with a felicitation and farewell meal my collaborators, my publisher Monsieur Hachette and a few friends from school days or thereabouts. Having become a sick man, I had to give up absolutely meetings and festive meals. I was hoping at first that this was nothing more than a postponement, but I hoped in vain. The postponement was definitive. Time improved nothing, it made everything worse; and, while writing these lines, I hold my pen with a hand that is weak and aching.

An incident apprised me early of the success that my book, once completed, was enjoying. Until then, the fascicles published one after the other had only very limited sales, a *succès d'estime*[†] but nothing beyond, according to many in my circle, who were also critics well-informed and well-disposed to me. And, in fact, the voluminous dimensions of the dictionary, its undoubtedly high price, and the scholarly character with which it was stamped seemed to prohibit access of the general public to it. However, the firm of Hachette had great hopes. I was rather, if only due to my fear of disappointment, on the side of wariness when, at Versailles, I was asked by Monsieur Carnot senior, my colleague in the National Assembly, how it was that one could not obtain a copy of my dictionary. To this question I had no reply, and I supposed that the bookseller whom Monsieur Carnot contacted had made some mistake. It was not the case. I was eager, you can well imagine, to enquire of Monsieur

---

[†]Success in the sense that the work is critically acclaimed, but not in a popular or commercial sense.

Hachette about it, who informed me that indeed from the outset the demand had exhausted whatever copies one had in stock, that he had been taken unawares, that he was glad of it, but that, from now on, a sufficient number of presses were running in full swing to fulfill the requirements. These presses no longer lacked work; and the publisher and the author witnessed regular sales. No doubt, the major part of these sales was and is still in France itself; nonetheless an important part, not to be despised, was accounted for by foreign countries. My dictionary has spread near and far; and from England in particular I received appreciations which profoundly touched me. I would not record this circumstance if it did not attest to the fact that the interest aroused by our language in the last two centuries, nay, in the Early Middle Ages, when our literature enjoyed already the favour of Europe, has not been lost, and that not only in our view, but also in the view of foreigners, we ought to care for our *parleüre* (it is the word used by our forbears); for *noblesse oblige.*

My dictionary was fully completed only at the end of my seventy-first year. The more I advanced in my old age, the greater my temerity became, and the further my chances of putting the finishing touches myself to the work decreased. My temerity had the upper hand. I was congratulated for this by one of my colleagues and friends, Laurent-Pichat, who supported my efforts, and helped my work. The expressions which he used have aroused in me the care to transcribe them; but I beg of my reader, who will certainly share this care, to forget their form and consider only the content: *'An illustrious man of our time'*, Laurent-Pichat said during a speech delivered at the prize-distribution in the Charlemagne High School on 5th August, 1879, *'whose moral heroism is before us as a great example, undertook an immense task, without thinking of the days that this life had in store for him. He commenced his work in his declining years. He worked at it for fifteen years; and the printing of his work also lasted perhaps about the same number of years. The endeavour was crowned with success; he raised a national monument; and be can repose now, while considering with serenity the edifice he has consecrated to the French language.'* These words, addressed to young boys who were entering life, about an old man who was leaving it, have seemed to me, despite the exaggeration of the praise, to deserve to be set down; especially since I know for certain that my example and my accompanying advice have encouraged more than one man of industry and action to look rather at what he had to do than what he had to live.

Supplementary note: The first pages of copy were delivered to the press on 27th September, 1859 and the closing ones on 4th July, 1872. The initial months of 1859 were spent on trials of types, with a packet of copy delivered for these trials.

The copy (without the *Supplement*) consisted of 415,636 leaves. There were 2,242 typeset galleys.

The additions made on the galleys produced 292 pages with three columns.

If the *Dictionary* (without the *Supplement*) were typeset on a single column, this column would measure 37,525.28 metres.

The typesetting commenced regularly in September 1859; the last galley (without the *Supplement*) was passed for plate on 14th November, 1872, which makes a duration of about thirteen years and two months.

The typesetting was interrupted only during the war, from 1st August, 1870 to 21st February, 1871, and during the Commune, from 19th April to 14th June, 1871.

ÉMILE LITTRÉ

BY

PIERRE LAROUSSE

MAXIMILIEN PAUL EMILE LITTRÉ, PHILOSOPHER, PHILOLOGIST AND POLITICIAN, BORN IN PARIS ON 1ST FEBRUARY, 1801. After leaving school, where his brilliant performance brought him to the fore, he studied medicine and became an intern. But, driven by his taste for literature, he soon gave up the practice of medicine to make an intensive study of the Greek language, and learn Arabic, Sanskrit and various other languages. Gifted with an inquiring and shrewd mind, Monsieur Littré, an indefatigable worker, addressed himself from then on to nearly the whole of the scientific field. Two years earlier, he had founded the *Journal hebdomadaire de medecine* ('Weekly Journal of Medicine'), with Messrs. Bouillaud, Andral, etc. Then the revolution of July 1830 broke out. Monsieur Littré, who even then belonged to the democratic party, was one of the combatants who dethroned Charles X. He joined, sometime later, the editorial staff of the *National,* of which he was one of the most distinguished collaborators until 1851. However, politics did not at all make him forget his scholarly and scientific work. In 1837, he founded with Dezeimeris a new medical journal, *l'Expérience*

('The Experiment'), and began, in 1839, the publication of his edition and his beautiful translation of the *Œuvres d'Hippocrate* ('Works of Hippocrates') (1839–1861, 10 Vols. 8vo.) which got him nominated, in the same year, to the *Académie des Inscriptions.* After the death of Fauviel (1844), this learned body designated him as member of the commission entrusted with continuing the *Histoire littéraire de Ia France* ('Literary History of France'). He was one of the main authors of vols. XXI, XXII and XXIII, and began then his long and profound research on the history of our language.

At this time Monsieur Littré was in contact with Auguste Comte, the founder of the philosophy of positivism, and had become one of his most fervent followers. His clear mind, in love with exactness, was captivated by the scientific character of this social and philosophical doctrine, to which we are devoting an article in its turn. Therefore, we shall say here only a few words, just to show the impassioned exaggeration present in the violent attacks made on Monsieur Littré, concerning his philosophical ideas. According to the positivist school, the history of the development of the human mind shows three essential phases, which correspond to three successive phases of civilisation. 'In the first, which is the theological phase', Monsieur Littré himself says, 'the explanation of things is linked to personalities who are the cause of the existences, phenomena and events. In the second, which constitutes the metaphysical phase, when criticism has begun to shake the spontaneous or theological ideas, a class of identity comes into play in the system and eliminates in increasing measure the divine beings whose agency had been admitted in every phenomenon. In the third, which is the positivist phase, the search for the Absolute, or in other words for primary causes and final causes, recognised from now onwards as inaccessible and good only for occupying the infancy of the human mind, is abandoned, and one applies oneself only to the search for laws and conditions.' Thus the philosophy of positivism abandons the search for the Absolute, whatever form it may take, either with respect to the origin of things, or with respect to their end and to their goal, because it is convinced that all search in this direction is useless. It does not deny the great metaphysical problems which, from time immemorial, have preoccupied the human mind; it confines itself to eliminating them from the scientific domain; it does not assert materialism, as has been repeatedly said, it says with Monsieur Littré: 'In the positive sciences, no property without matter is recognised, not because, *a priori*, one has a preconceived idea that there exists no independent spiritual substance, but because, *a posteriori*, one has never encountered gravitation without a heavy body, heat without a hot body, electricity without an electrical substance, affinity without substance of combination, life, feeling and thought without a living, feeling and thinking being.' That these doctrines might have appeared to be disputable from the philosophical and social points of view is a question that we do not have to examine here; what is incontestable is that, employed in the sciences of reasoning and observation, in the political and literary history, they have given excellent results, and that Monsieur Littré himself has applied them with the greatest success to his studies on the French language.

Monsieur Littré remained for a long time the disciple of Comte, and during this period, as he has told us himself, he frequently put forward, under his direct inspiration, doctrines for which he was sharply criticised, and which moreover he has abandoned since. When Comte threw himself into mystical ideas, and wanted to add a theurgical system to his doctrines, Monsieur Littré parted company with him, and, ever since the death of the master, he has remained the head of the positivist school which has not followed what has been termed the doctrinal deviations of the aged Comte.

During the revolution of February 1848, Monsieur Littré became member of the municipal council of Paris; but, from the end of the same year, he went back totally to his research. In 1854 he joined the editorial office of the *Journal des savants* ('Journal of Scientists'), to which he contributed a large number of articles, and founded, in 1857, the *Revue de philosophie positive* ('Review of Positivist Philosophy'), which he has been editing ever since. In 1863, he began the publication of his major work, his *Dictionnaire de la langue française* ('Dictionary of the French

Language') (2 large volumes), completed nine years later, in December 1872. We have spoken of this vast and learned work, this beautiful philological monument, at page 16 of the preface to the *Grand Dictionnaire Universel du XIXe siècle* (1864–1884) ('Great Universal Dictionary of the 19th Century')[1]. In the same year, 1863, Monsieur Littré put himself up as a candidate for the *Academie française,* but a vicious tract, in which the fiery bishop Dupanloup denounced his doctrines as immoral and impious, prevented him from getting elected. Even while unrelentingly busy with his *Dictionnaire,* the indefatigable scholar contributed to the *Revue de la philosophie positive* numerous remarkable studies, of which, especially, the one entitled *Des origines organiques de la morale* ('The Organic Origins of Morals') (January, 1870), caused considerable stir, and drew fresh attacks on him. Shortly thereafter, when Madame Comte filed a suit against the executors of her husband's will, with the intention of preventing them from publishing the last writings of Auguste Comte, as being unworthy of him, Monsieur Littré put himself

---

[1]In this preface, Pierre Larousse criticises the etymologies of Littré, which he judges as incomplete (Larousse gives Sanskritic etymology). In fact, Larousse writes freely without the constraint of length. The second criticism is directed at the typographical arrangement, like the absence of indentation. 'Some paragraphs', he says, 'have two, three, four or five hundred lines. The examples have nothing which distinguishes them from the text of the definition; verses appear in the form and characters of prose.' In most of the new editions, these defects do not exist any more.

on the side of the widow, and strongly supported the legitimacy of her demand. When the German armies marched on Paris in September 1870, Monsieur Littré, nearly seventy, had to withdraw to the province at the insistence of his friends. He retired to Bordeaux, and Monsieur Gambetta[†], who had reorganised the *École Polytechnique* in that town, called upon him to occupy a chair of history and geography therein (7th January, 1871).

Elected Deputy for the province of Seine to the National Assembly on 8th December, 1871 by 87,686 votes, Monsieur Littré took his seat on the benches to the Left, among the Republicans. He voted in favour of the preliminaries for peace, of the disbanding of the national guards, against the repeal of the laws concerning exile, against the validation of the elections of the princes of Orleans, for the return of the Assembly to Paris, etc., and constantly supported by his votes the policy of Thiers. Utterly lacking in oratorical skills, he took no part in the discussions of the Chamber, but frequently voiced his opinion on the questions on the agenda through articles, published either in the *Revue positive*, or in various dailies, inspired by a spirit of extreme moderation. We shall cite notably those which he published on the partial re-elections to the Assembly, of which he declared himself to be in favour (November 1871), on the policy to be

---

[†]One of the founders of the Third Republic.

followed in our position as the vanquished (March 1872), on the condition of France in 1872 (August 1872), on the relationship of the Assembly with universal suffrage (January, 1873), on learning the ways and means of founding the Republic, the only government possible (May 1873), etc. A powerful wind animates these pages. The criminal Empire of 2nd December, with its scandals and failures, is hauled to the pillory of history, with forceful and patriotic indignation.

On 15th October, 1871, Monsieur Littré was elected member of the Municipal Council of the province of Seine for the canton of Saint-Denis, and later vice-president of the Council. On 30th December of the same year, despite all the efforts of Monsieur Dupanloup, the French Academy decided at last to admit him, and elected him in replacement of Villemain. The hotheaded bishop of Orleans was so annoyed by this that he immediately gave his resignation as academician with great fanfare. In his speech as a new member (5th June, 1873), Monsieur Littré abstained from all philosophical controversy and spoke only of literature, and made a remarkable panegyric of the French language of the 12th century. Less prudent, the obscure Monsieur de Champagny, entrusted with the responsibility of responding to him, assumed the presumptuous task of sermonising his illustrious colleague, and addressed to the master of positivist philosophy such a homily as would certainly not have been disowned by Monsieur Dupanloup.

Monsieur Littré is one of the most educated men of our time, one of the worthiest representatives of liberty, science, and the independence of human reason, and a first-rate linguist. 'He is', said Sainte-Beuve, 'a man of science, method, comparison, reason, vigour, and even rigour, nourished with the bread of the great of all kinds, with the generous sap of the doctrines, all spirit and all energy.' Monsieur Scherer said on his part: 'Monsieur Littré has written excellent pages, without ever having sought to write a page. One feels that the subtleties of the academic language, the affected and pretentious refinements, are not in his line. His criticism does not soar in flight. It penetrates more than it travels, it goes straight to the heart of things.'

Besides the works already cited, we owe to this scholar *le Cholera oriental* ('The Oriental Cholera') (1832, 8vo); the translation of the *Vie de Jesus* ('Life of Jesus') by Dr Strauss (Paris, 1839 – 40, 2 vols. 8vo); *La poésie homérique et l'ancienne poésie française* ('Homeric Poetry and the Old French Poetry'), an ingenious and scholarly study, published in *Revue des Deux-mondes* (1st July, 1847), where one finds the translation of the first book of the *Iliad* in 13th century French; *Histoire naturelle de Pline* ('Natural History of Pliny') (1848, 2vols. 8vo) translated for the Latin classics collection of Nisard; *Application de la philosophie positive au gouvernement des sociétés, et en particulier à la crise actuelle* ('Application of the Positivist Philosophy to the Government of the Societies, and in Particular to the Present Crisis') (1849, 8vo); *Conservation, politique et positivisme* ('Conservation, Politics and Positivism') (1852, 12mo); *Sur la Mort de M. Auguste Comte* ('On the Death of Monsieur Auguste Comte') (1857, 8vo); *Paroles de philosophie positive* ('Words of Positivist Philosophy') (1859, 8vo), a résumé of the positivist doctrine; *Histoire de la langue française* ('History of the French Language') (1862, 2 vols. 8vo), a collection of articles on the old language; *Auguste Comte et la philosophie positive* ('Auguste Comte and the Positivist Philosophy') (1863, 8vo); *Médecine et médecins* ('Medicine and Doctors') (1872, 8vo); *la Science au point de vue philosophique* ('Science from the Philosophical Point of View') (1873, 8vo), etc. Lastly, we owe to him an edition of *Les* (Œuvres complètes d'Armand Carrel') ('The Complete Works of Armand Carrel') (1857), and a revised edition of the *Dictionnaire de médecine de Nysten* ('Nysten's Dictionary of Medicine') in collaboration with Monsieur Robin. It is in this dictionary that one finds the scientific definition of man, which has been the subject of so much ridiculous outcry and grotesque indignation.

AFTERWORD

BY

JACQUES CELLARD

'A national monument...' However much aware of the merits of his dictionary he may have been, Émile Littré could himself scarcely call it that. It is one thing to be legitimately proud of a work well-accomplished, and crowned with success; quite another to 'pantheonise'† oneself one's work. Our author does it all the same, by resorting to an old man's ruse: these words of praise, he says, were uttered by another. I am only reporting them, even if this other happens to be, by sheer chance, a collaborator and a friend.

It is still true that the *Dictionnaire de la langue française* is certainly a national monument as claimed by its author. The eulogy is double-edged: a monument is 'what endures' and also 'what is dated'. The Littré dictionary has lasted for well over a century; and its more or less faithful editions, which are published ever since it became public property, prove that this success has not flagged.

---

†*Panthéon* is a monument dedicated to the great men of France. Inclusion among the illustrious persons honoured there is the ultimate recognition.

Its compilation, begun in 1845, continued, including the *Supplement*, until 1875. Other dictionaries of the language, that of Paul Robert, for example, have been many times 'revised, corrected and enlarged', to cite the usual formula. The will of the heirs of Littré has maintained his dictionary in its exact original form, *tel qu'en lui-même enfin...* †

So, in this condition, the collection of attestations scarcely goes beyond the 1860's, in the best of cases. The *Supplement*, it is true, extends this date up to 1875, and its modernity is remarkable: but who consults the *Supplement?* Who even suspects its range? And who, conversely in some manner, takes a proper measure of the archaeological richness of *Littré?* It was somewhat hastily said of his etymological explanations that they were worthless, and, in any case, out of date; therefore, the present day republications 'forget' them.

This process is absurd. It was an etymological project that Émile Littré and Louis Hachette started in 1841; five years later, this project was extended to the historical origin of the words and then to their grammar. At no time did the author lose sight of the main direction of his enterprise, and, in his view, its real *raison d'être*: to construct a history of words through texts. Before

---

†Allusion to the opening line of Stéphane Mallarmé's poem: *Tombeau d'Edgar Poe* ('Tomb of Edgar Poe'):

Tel qu'en Lui-même enfin l'éternité le change,

Such as into himself at last Eternity changes him,

any other instrumental role, the Littré dictionary is a superb anthology of nine centuries of our literature and our history.

This plan, very much in conformity with the genius of our nation, will be subsequently that of the two great successors of the Littré dictionary: The *Robert* dictionary, which no longer needs introduction, and the *Trésor de la Langue Française* ('Thesaurus of the French Language'), compiled at Nancy by a team of the CNRS†, which is being published. In both of these, the 'anthological' aspect of the work is very well highlighted by the typography: the citations-attestations are clearly separated from the commentary. Their variety and their beauty are therefore perfectly obvious to the eye.

Littré, alas, was working under very different technical and commercial conditions. Getting bigger and bigger as the years went by, the dictionary required, from Louis Hachette, ever-increasing amounts of capital, resulting in a sale price to the public that ran the risk of being 'dissuasive'. It was necessary, therefore, to pare down the costs absolutely, that is to say, as much in respect of paper as of typesetting. That is why the Littré dictionary, composed in three columns (as against two, with the same format, for the Robert and the Thesaurus of the French Language) is in very small characters, and is difficult to read.

---

†*Centre National de la Recherche Scientifique* (National Centre for Scientific Research).

That is why above all, within each entry, the citations follow immediately after the definition, in the same type, with nothing to distinguish, in the entry or in the sub-entry, the part of the lexicographer-commentator from the part of the author-illustrator. Add to this the fact that a considerable portion of the illustrations-citations is drawn from poetic works; and that the verse, typeset immediately following the definition, is really indistinguishable from it. The greatest part of the very real literary beauty of the dictionary therefore escapes our notice for material, and fortuitous, reasons.

This problem of space confronted the lexicographers and their publishers at an early date. The *Académie française* had devised a solution for it in 1694, which has never been reconsidered afterwards. Its plan comprised two parallel dictionaries of the French language. In one, the words of the general vocabulary would be dealt with in detail: in the other the professional terms – the technical vocabulary – would be treated more briefly. The awkward question was, and still remains, that a large number of general words are at the same time technical terms, and *vice-versa.*

But the drawback of a single dictionary is no less. Of the 120,000 entries, or thereabouts, of the Littré dictionary (*Supplement* included), how many belong, or have belonged, only to the vocabulary of a profession, or to a technique that has become quickly outdated? How many deserve no linguistic or stylistic commentary? The mixed object thus created aims to be at the same time a dictionary of the language and an encyclopaedia; and is truly neither the one nor the other. The commercial argument, maximising the number of entries of a dictionary of language, proves inevitably to be prejudicial to the semantic quality.

'If the dictionary', Littré himself says with naive enthusiasm, 'were typeset in a single column, this column would measure 37,525.28 metres'. What of it? Of course, this concern for quantifying – always more! – is inherent in lexicographic activity. But the nineteenth century saw its apotheosis: the accumulation of words, therefore of knowledge, is for the society of that time a clear transposition of the accumulation of capital, and therefore of power. In this sense the Littré dictionary is always to our language what the Eiffel Tower still is to our industry: a retrospective showcase of the national genius.

So here we are back to our monument behind which, in the self-portrait which the present text is, stands the man Littré. Here two images are superimposed and intermingled indistinguishably: that of a man effectively, Maximilien Paul Émile, 1801–1881, physician, philosopher, good citizen, good husband, good father; and that of a personage, or rather of an almost caricatural personification of all the virtues of the lay saint of the 19th century. Positivist agnostic, Littré has been for his contemporaries, and remains for us, the living proof that an irreproachable moral has no need, to support itself, of any other belief than the faith in the continuous progress of the human mind.

We have shaken off somewhat these generous illusions. There still remains, in our man, an 'assault course' which compels admiration. *How* I *Made My Dictionary,* Littré's account of the genesis of his dictionary, happily reissued now, is at the same time an investigation report and the narrative of an ascetic adventure which resembles more the *Spiritual Exercises* of Ignatius Loyola than the *Confessions* of Jean-Jacques Rousseau. This ascetic will is expressed first of all, as in the founder of the Jesuits, by an implacable rigour in the management of irreplaceable time. A few hours, each day, are devoted to sleeping and eating; a few others, each Sunday, to rare friends. All the rest is devoted to the all-consuming dictionary. The domestic life of the Littrés, father, mother and daughter, is of an equally ascetic frugality: the family lives, during twenty years, on the advances agreed to by the publisher, at the rate of ... 200 francs per month. It is in those days the salary of a petty clerk in the Railways. And Littré is by then a scholar of international repute!

The machinery so assembled, for the best part, from 1845, is not safe from History, which strikes first in 1848: a riot soon transformed into a revolution ruins Littré, who from then on considers it a conscientious obligation to work still more to reimburse his publisher. There was an even more intense alarm in 1870. The 240,000 leaves of Littré's manuscript escape the Prussians only to run the greater risk of being burnt by the men of the Commune, for whom, despite his being quite liberal and quite republican, Littré has no kind word.

An exemplary life? The question is necessarily askew. Émile Littré's life appears to be as little affected by human weaknesses as if he had been a Benedictine monk of the twelfth century; probably even less. But what would be a society of Benedictines even if non-religious? His exemplariness appears to us therefore to be of a different kind: it is in the absolute coherence between the temperament and the project. The constant and violent tension which Littré imposes on himself during seventy years (for he seems never to have had a 'youth') to accomplish an immense work appears without doubt superhuman to all others; it is to him but the reasoned exercise of the faculties which Nature gave him. This exercise finds in itself its own justification. It is not a question of working for the greatest glory of God, or even for the great relief of others, but 'of exhausting what is possible'; if need be by starting work, for keeping busy during the last days of one's life, on 'a universal history for which I had the complete plan'.

There is here something heroic and burlesque-like at the same time. What author of a dictionary is sure of preserving always his good sense? Lexicography is not a mad-man's profession, to be sure: it requires too much of method and clarity of mind. But it is, on occasion, a profession which drives one mad.